D0983599

★ SPORTS STARS ★

JIM ABBOTT

ALL-AMERICAN PITCHER

By Howard Reiser

CHILDRENS PRESS ®
CHICAGO

Picture Acknowledgments

Cover, Sports Chrome East/West; 6, New York Yankees; 9, AP/Wide World; 13, 14, *The Flint Journal,* Flint, Michigan; 16, UPI/Bettmann; 19, *The Flint Journal,* Flint, Michigan; 21, 23, Focus On Sports; 24, Reuters/Bettmann; 27, AP/Wide World; 29, UPI/Bettmann; 31, Focus On Sports; 32, 33, AP/Wide World; 35, 36, ©John Cordes/California Angels; 37, Wide World Photos; 39, ©Rich Kane/Sports Chrome East/West; 40, Focus On Sports; 43, AP/Wide World; 47, ©V. J. Lovero/California Angels

Project Editor: Shari Joffe
Design: Beth Herman Design Associates
Photo Research: Jan Izzo

Reiser, Howard.
    Jim Abbott (All-American pitcher) / by Howard Reiser.
      p. cm.–(Sports stars)
    Summary: Discusses the life and career of a major-league baseball player who has only one hand.
    ISBN 0-516-04376-5
    1. Abbott, Jim, 1967- –Juvenile literature. 2. Baseball players–United States–Biography–Juvenile literature. [1. Abbott, Jim, 1967- . 2. Baseball players. 3. Physically handicapped.] I. Title. II. Series.
GV865.A26R45   1993
796.357'092–dc20   93-7424
[B]   CIP
                                    AC

JIM ABBOTT

ALL-AMERICAN PITCHER

He is one of the best young pitchers in the major leagues. He is only the fifteenth player in the history of baseball to go directly to the major leagues without spending any time in the minors. He set a major-league record for most games won by a rookie pitcher. He happened to be born without a right hand.

Jim Abbott receives hundreds of letters every week. Many are written by children who have disabilities, or their parents. Jim tries to answer each letter. He is happy to boost the spirits of others and offer encouragement. However, he has never considered himself a hero, or deserving of special praise.

"I do not believe that I should be looked upon as anything special, merely because I was born with one hand," Jim says. "Everyone has challenges to overcome. You simply must work hard to reach your goal and to achieve success."

Jim was one of the most popular players on the California Angels. He expected to remain with the Angels for many years. However, on December 6, 1992, he was traded to the New York Yankees for three young prospects.

"I was shocked by the trade," Jim admits. "I found it difficult to take." But Abbott felt better after speaking to Yankees manager Buck Showalter a day after the trade was made.

"Buck assured me that the Yankees were committed to winning, just as I am," said Abbott. "He told me the Yankees were determined to finish in first place. Buck said I would be a very important part of the team. I began to feel excited about pitching for the Yankees, and being on the same team with such a great player as Don Mattingly."

Jim (left) was traded to the New York Yankees in 1992, after he played four seasons with the California Angels.

———————— ★ ★ ★ ————————

James Anthony Abbott was born in Flint, Michigan, on September 19, 1967. He was a beautiful baby. For some reason, he was born without a right hand.

Jim's parents, Mike and Kathy, were both only eighteen years old when Jim was born. Understandably, they were concerned about their son. They knew that having a disability would be a challenge for him. But they loved him very much, and were determined to provide a healthy, happy household for him. As one reporter has said about Jim's parents, "They raised a remarkable boy by never treating him too remarkably."

"My parents always encouraged me to play with other children and to participate in activities that I enjoyed," Jim says. "They always supported me. They felt I could accomplish whatever I set my mind to doing. And, as a youngster, I often dreamed of pitching in the major leagues."

Although they encouraged Jim, Mike and Kathy knew that children were sometimes cruel to him. There were incidents that the Abbott family will never forget. Mike and Kathy recall that one day, when Jim was five years old, he came home from school crying. "I am not going to wear this anymore," Jim said, pointing to the steel hook he had been fitted with to use as an artificial hand. Jim had reason to be upset. At school, some thoughtless kids had called him "Mr. Hook." His parents understood Jim's anger and frustration. They agreed to let him stop wearing his artificial hand.

As a child, Jim often played ball with his father and his younger brother, Chad. "I loved playing ball," Jim recalls. "My having one hand was not a big issue when I was a kid. I never gave thought to having one hand."

He began playing little league when he was eleven years old. In his first game, he pitched a no-hitter. He soon proved he could also field.

Many batters tried to reach base against Abbott by bunting the ball. But Jim would use his quickness to throw out the runners.

He later showed his fielding skills as a pitcher at Flint Central High School. Once, the other team bunted against him eight straight times. Jim threw out the last seven batters. "Jim was one of our best fielders," recalls Jim's high-school coach, Bob Holec.

Jim developed his fielding style at a young age, with help from his father. While delivering the ball, he rests his glove on his right wrist. After releasing the ball, he completes his follow-through by slipping his left hand into the glove so he is prepared to field the ball. After catching the ball, Jim quickly tucks the glove under his right arm, removes the ball from his glove, and throws.

Jim began playing little league when he was eleven years old.

Jim was an outstanding high-school pitcher.

In 1945, the Saint Louis Browns had an outfielder named Pete Gray who had one arm. Gray played at a time when many players were serving in World War II. Even with only one arm, he earned a major-league batting average of .218. But Gray lasted in the big leagues for only one season.

Abbott had read about Gray. But he did not wish to be compared to him. "I wanted to be another Nolan Ryan, not another Pete Gray," Abbott says.

Jim enjoyed an outstanding athletic career at Flint Central. He won fourteen games against only seven losses during his sophomore and junior years. As a senior, he won ten games, lost three, pitched three no-hitters, batted .427, hit seven home runs, and drove in thirty-six runs. He was selected to the All-State team.

Nor were his athletic skills restricted to baseball. As a senior, he was one of Michigan's best high-school quarterbacks, leading his team to the semifinals of the state championship. Recalling his school days, Abbott said, "Everyone was involved in athletics at Flint. There was a tremendous spirit."

Despite his success as a high-school pitcher, Jim sometimes became discouraged when he did not pitch well. "We never pressured him, but we explained that even the best pitchers did not always win," said Jim's mother. "Jim learned to understand that you have to accept the disappointments."

Abbott was always well-liked by others. People responded to his broad smile, modest manner, and friendly personality. As a high-school student, Jim even became a local sports celebrity. Younger kids, especially, looked up to him. Many asked for his autograph. Jim's sincerity and kind words always made them feel good.

Meanwhile, Jim's pitching talent—and potential—were making baseball scouts feel good. As Jim prepared to graduate from high school, the Toronto Blue Jays of the American League chose him in the thirty-sixth round of the baseball draft. Jim was offered $50,000 to sign a contract. However, he was also considering a baseball scholarship offered him by the University of Michigan. Jim had rooted for Michigan's baseball team for as long as he could remember.

While Jim considered his decision, his mother offered a clue. "We have tried to instill in Jim the importance of an education," she told reporters. A short while later, Abbott announced that he would attend the University of Michigan. He would get an education first, and hope that the major leagues would still be interested in him when he was finished.

In 1985, Jim accepted a baseball scholarship from the University of Michigan.

When Jim arrived on campus in the fall of
1985, he was filled with pride. "I would not trade
places with anyone in the world," he announced.

Jim got off to a poor start at the beginning of
the baseball season. But coach Bud Middaugh
was not concerned. He knew that the large
number of reporters covering Abbott's every
move was making it difficult for his young
pitcher to concentrate. "He will settle down,"
predicted Middaugh.

Middaugh was right. Jim soon won his first
game, in relief. (Jim is ordinarily a starting
pitcher, but on that occasion, he entered the
game as a reliever.) He went on to compile a
record of six wins and two losses, and made only
one error all season. He was voted to the Big Ten
Play-offs All-Tournament Team.

Jim talking with one of his college coaches

Jim followed up his freshman season with
a terrific sophomore year. He won eleven
games, lost three, and had an earned run
average of 2.03. At one point, he pitched thirty-
five straight innings without giving up an
earned run.

And once again, Jim's fielding was excellent. He made only two errors all year. "I am amazed by how well he can field," marveled California Angels scout Bob Gardner.

Jim's popularity grew. "People say I am courageous," he acknowledged. "But I do not pitch to be courageous. I pitch to win, just like any pitcher."

Abbott's skill as a pitcher earned him a special honor that summer. He was asked to be a member of the United States team that would play in the 1987 Pan-American Games. This international event, held every four years, includes such sports as baseball, basketball, and gymnastics.

Team USA, as the American team was called, set off on a tour to prepare for the Pan-Am Games. Abbott pitched extremely well during the tour. He won six games against one loss and had an earned run average of 1.70. In July, when the team was in Cuba, Jim became a hero by being the first American pitcher to win a game against Cuba in twenty-five years. "They will be talking about Jim Abbott many years from now," predicted Team USA head coach Ron Fraser, after Jim's three-hit win over Cuba.

The Pan-American Games began on August 8, 1987, in Indianapolis, Indiana. Jim carried the American flag at the opening ceremonies. "It was a tremendous thrill," he recalls.

Jim experienced both disappointment and satisfaction during the competition. He was disappointed by Team USA's loss to Cuba in the finals. But he was proud about having won two games in three appearances, thereby helping the United States win a silver medal. His earned run average during the games was an amazing 0.00.

In the fall of 1987, Jim won the United States Baseball Federation's Golden Spikes Award, presented annually to the best amateur baseball player in America. A few months later, Jim received an even greater honor. At an awards dinner on March 7, 1988, he was named the winner of the coveted Sullivan Award, presented to the best amateur athlete in the United States. No baseball player had ever won the award. "I am completely in shock," Jim said upon receiving the award.

1987
DEN SPIKE ARD
SPONSORED BY

1987
GOLDEN SPIKES
AWARD

Jim Abbott was now the most famous college baseball player in America. The University of Michigan baseball team was to begin its season only four days after Jim won the Sullivan Award. Anxious to prove that he deserved the award, Jim put too much pressure upon himself. As a result, he got off to a poor start.

It wasn't long, however, before he began pitching well. Jim finished the 1988 season with nine wins and three losses, and made *The Sporting News* All-America team.

Jim was expected to be selected high in the major-league draft that June. Yet some teams still doubted whether a pitcher with one hand could properly field his position.

In 1988, Jim won the Sullivan Award, presented annually to the most outsanding amateur athlete in America.

The California Angels, though, were confident in Jim's ability. They drafted him in the first round. "He can field," insisted Angels scout George Bradley. "He's also the most talented pitcher that we have seen out there."

During the summer, Jim's performance as a pitcher continued to draw raves. After being invited to join the 1988 United States Olympic baseball team, he traveled to Seoul, Korea. There, in the final game of the baseball competition, he pitched the American team to a gold-medal victory over the defending Olympic champions, the Japanese team. "This is the greatest sports thrill I ever had," Jim said after the Olympic victory.

At the 1988 Olympics, Jim was the winning pitcher in the game that clinched the gold medal for the U.S. team.

Jim warming up for a game

Jim chatting with reporters in the Angel's locker room

Jim reported to the Angels training camp in Mesa, Arizona, on February 15, 1989. From the beginning, he was surrounded by reporters and television camera crews. "He's answered some of the dumbest questions I have ever heard," remarked manager Doug Rader. "He's handled everything with dignity."

Early in spring training, catcher Lance Parrish praised Abbott. "Jim has as strong an arm as any lefthander I have ever caught," said Parrish.

Despite the compliments, Abbott was slated to pitch in the Angels minor-league system that summer. After all, in the previous twenty-four years, only nine pitchers had made the jump to the major leagues without minor-league experience.

But it soon became clear that Jim could help the Angels immediately. His blazing fastball, hard slider, and fine curve earned him the respect of batters. Shortly before the season began, the Angels announced that Abbott would be placed on their major-league roster.

Jim won his first big-league game on April 24, 1989, against the Baltimore Orioles. In May, he pitched a shutout against Roger Clemens and the Boston Red Sox. He went on to compile a season record of twelve wins and twelve losses. His twelve wins were the most ever achieved by a professional rookie pitcher. He was also voted to Topps's All-Star Rookie team.

Jim appreciates the support he receives from his fans.

Although his popularity soared, Jim sometimes got tired of reporters continually asking about his disability. He wanted to be recognized simply for what he accomplished on the field, not for the fact that he doesn't have a right hand. "I never doubted my ability to pitch with one hand," he said. "I do not have to be like everyone else to be happy."

Jim soon developed into a great major-league pitcher.

In his four years with the Angels, Jim certainly was not like everyone else. Even though his record was forty-seven wins against fifty-two losses, he was still one of the best pitchers in the league. Often, he had failed to receive strong batting support from his teammates. For example, in 1992, his record was seven wins and fifteen losses; but his earned run average was 2.77 runs per game, the fifth best in the league. And, for the third straight year, he pitched more than two hundred innings.

Jim leaps to catch a line drive.

Jim Abbott had another reason to be happy: in December 1991, he got married. His wife, Dana, is an athlete as well. Dana played basketball at the University of California at Irvine.

Abbott would like to be the Yankees's top pitcher in the years to come. "I have always respected the number-one pitchers," Jim said. "There are certain guys who consistently pitch well. They rise to the top every year. I would like to be one of those pitchers."

Buck Showalter feels that Abbott can attain this goal. "I have always respected Jim Abbott's talent, determination, and commitment to hard work," said the Yankees manager shortly before the start of spring training. "I expect him to be a major pitching force, and make a big contribution to the success of our club."

Says California Angels coach Ron Carew: "Jim could easily be a twenty-game winner for the Yankees. He's got the ability, a well as the determination. He's got what it takes to make it big."

Jim Abbott has been a winner all his life. But his victories go beyond his accomplishments on the baseball field. Jim Abbott is a winner because of his courage, his character, and the example he sets for others. "People think of me as an underdog," Jim once remarked. "But I have always thought of myself as a ballplayer!"

Jim Abbott is a ballplayer all right—he's one of the best. But he is more than a ballplayer. He is a sensitive, caring person, whose words of encouragement have helped to provide hope and inspiration to many others.

"Always try to do the best you can," Jim advises children. "If you work hard, you can accomplish any goal you set for yourself. Nothing is impossible. You can do it!"

Jim offers another very important message. "Always be kind and friendly to others," he says. "Treat everyone with respect. Treat others as you wish to be treated yourselves."

Not only does Jim Abbott pitch like a champion, but he also acts like a champion. For this, he deserves a standing ovation from everyone, not just from baseball fans.

Chronology

1967 – James Anthony Abbott, the son of Mike and Kathy Abbott, is born in Flint, Michigan, on September 19.

1979 – Jim pitches a no-hitter in his first little-league game.

1984 – Jim is one of best high-school quarterbacks in Michigan. He leads Flint Central High School to the semifinals of the state football championship.

1985 – In his senior year of high school, Jim wins ten games, loses three, pitches three no-hitters, and bats .427.

– Jim accepts a baseball scholarship from the University of Michigan.

1986 – Jim is voted to the Big Ten Play-offs All-Tournament team.

1987 – As a sophomore, Jim wins eleven games, loses three, and makes only two errors.

– As a member of Team USA, Jim carries the American flag at the opening ceremonies of the Pan-American Games in Indianapolis. He helps Team USA win a silver medal at the games.

– Jim wins the Golden Spikes Award, presented to the best amateur baseball player in America.

1988 – Jim wins the Sullivan Award, given to the best amateur athlete in America.

– Jim is named to *The Sporting News* All-America Team.

– Jim is drafted in the first round of the major-league baseball draft by the California Angels.

– As a member of the U.S. Olympic baseball team at the Summer Olympics in Seoul, Korea, Jim is the winning pitcher in the game against Japan that earns the gold medal for the U.S. team.

1989 – After an impressive spring training, Jim is assigned to the California Angels roster without ever having pitched in the minor leagues.

– Jim wins his first major-league game April 24, against the Baltimore Orioles. He wins twelve games during the season, the most ever won by a big-league rookie pitcher.

1990 – Jim pitches $211\frac{2}{3}$ innings, the first of three straight years of his pitching more than 200 innings for the Angels.

1992 – Jim's earned run average is 2.77 runs per game, the fifth best in the American League.

– Jim is traded to the New York Yankees.

About the Author

Howard Reiser has been well-known New York City newspaper reporter, columnist, and bureau chief. He has also worked as a labor news writer and editor. Today a political speechwriter, Mr. Reiser covered the major news stories in New York City for more than twenty-five years.

Mr. Reiser has written several other books for the *Sports Stars* series, including *Nolan Ryan, Scottie Pippen,* and *Barry Sanders.* He and his wife, Adrienne, live in New York. They have four children: Philip, Helene, Steven, and Stuart.